ACKNOWLEDGEMENTS

Thanks are due to Nigel McLoughlin and acknowledgements are due to the editors of the following journals and publications, in which some of the sections of this sequence first appeared individually:

The Antigonish Review (Canada),
*Poetry Monthly International, Purple Patch,
Reversion, Treasures of the Unconscious*.

CONTENTS

WHO I AM

John and Willie John McGrath, binding corn, c.1961

Niall McGrath

Belfast
LAPWING

First Published by Lapwing Publications
c/o 1, Ballysillan Drive
Belfast BT14 8HQ
lapwing.poetry@ntlworld.com
http://www.freewebs.com/lapwingpoetry/

Since before 1632
The Greig sept of the MacGregor Clan
Has been printing and binding books

All Lapwing Publications are
Hand-printed and Hand-bound in Belfast
Set in Aldine 721 BT at the Winepress

ISBN 978-1-907276-23-1

ii

DEDICATION

To:

my mother, my sons
and any future generation

Mrs Patton, Stranocum, Cassie's mother, c.1920s
(see page 37).

I

BEYOND THE MEMORY OF MAN...

Gamekeeper's Lodge on Belfast's Black Mountain, c. 1940s
(see page 40).

I.   GENESIS

Beyond the memory of man...
Whiteness. Emptiness.
Comfort giving way to
chill. Contentment transfiguring
in another pattern as permafrost
becomes slush and bog,
dries to meadow and drumlin.
Saplings stretch in brightness.
Barrenness eases to temperate;
overcomes aridity. Branches droop,
drops quench loam and peat.

Tribes spread from the dark heart,
where the survivors dwelt.
An oligarch of adventurers stray:
encamps where undisturbed
salmon leap, deer and hare hop, wolf stalks.
They clear pastures, turn soil
to cultivate strips of fodder.
From the east: seed that spreads
rampant crops across the land.
A foothold is secured;
the island of youth is explored.

II.   EXPULSION

Like dolmens round my childhood, the old people...
Nomads, settling in a valley of plenty.
One son tills soil, produces wholesome grain,
the other corrals livestock,
supplies neighbours' lust for comfort.
He is bestowed with the riches he craves,
regardless of the karma they carry.
Be careful what you wish for...
Righteous anger overspills,
spills blood.
Repentant, self-loathing exiles
the agriculturalist
amongst untouchables.

Relishing newfound ease,
the parents are distracted from
their sorrow and from their goal,
indulge in the carnal,
no longer see each other
as two halves of the same kernel.
They snatch time selfishly,
fret over appearances;
sup the juices of the vine
till their faces are bloated red as the earth,
red as their offspring's blood
fertilising the once virgin garden.
And so paradise eludes them, too;
banishment prevails.

III.   DELUGE

Wandering Burren-like wilderness,
a man senses the earth's trepidation,
the sky's sullenness, the wind's moodiness.
He builds himself a freestanding *crannóg*,
a vessel in which to ride out the fluctuating tide
with kith, kin, useful creatures.
Waters drown the land.
These survivors of catastrophe
are forced to devour the flesh
of cloven-hoofed beasts
until the plains are productive again.
By which time they have the taste of blood,
like dogs driven wild by the scent of blood
they keep returning to tear the throats
of innocent creatures.
Each night the spits turn
above flames leaping like
serpent's tongues to lick
fat dripping from roasting flesh.
There is no end to the holocaust.

IV.   OF KINGS AND COUNTRY

Where blood is split, tribal justice prevails;
order emanates from the strong.
Of these, in one province rises,
from the princely caste, Kennedy.
Still the wolves roam, though snakes
have long since been banished.
And with the north wind sweeps
terror – steel flashing
beneath blazing torch or fierce sun.
The rampant quest of hunger stalks;
the decree of greed stamps -
moving his thighs
like an upraised bull -
among its victims, a band of brothers,
including the Horse Lord.
Only the heir and bairn escape
to stand another day.

V.   AFTER THE HORSE LORD

Disparate settlements have been named
in honour of this Celtic prince so famed...

Brian's brother Ectigern begot
ten tribes, both Irish and Scot:
McGovern, McCloy, McKennedy, Eachan,
Heffernan, Cafferty, Stead, Steadman,
Ahern and the sons of Craith.

Aughrim, Aughinish, Duneight, Donaghanie,
Eachlein, Lemanagh, Leamanach, Tuaghy,
Eochaidh's Lake, Ballymackilough, Strachan
and Keoghville commemorate the man;
all these places and all the clans McGrath.

VI.   HOLY LAND

Sixmilebridge to Sixmilewater their domain,
across provinces and generations.
This is the land of lovers and saints:
the country where desire hangs on the air
like apples on the crabtree, waiting to be plucked
or falling to the ground, to be snatched
and carried off to some chieftain's lair
or some devotee's cell, where they count
and store each salvaged fruit with care,
awaiting the feast day with such great hunger.

This is the land of the all-attractive diva:
where clansmen training in hilltop forts,
farmers ploughing in valley meadows,
craftsmen sweating in crossroads forges,
sailors aboard their lilting boats,
druids counselling the afflicted in forest glades,
millers grinding in glens and gorges,
all pine for a glimpse from earthly shadows
of the elusive Macha
before the shimmering vision fades.

VII.   DIASPORA

As autumn scatters twigs and leaves,
deposits acorns in carpets
of gold and mauve, they disperse,
tentatively root,
wait the long winters through
until new sunshine
blesses each straining circle of growth.
Trees burgeon.

VIII.   KEEPERS OF THE LOUGH

Our approach through copse
is shrouded in mist, cold,
interminable loanens that confuse,
each resembling every other backroad.
That Sunday morning stillness.
Chill across the lough.
Sharpness. Clarity. Brightness.
Ferryboat moving as lightly as a *corrach*.

Mumblings as beads clack.
Bells echo off cornflower sky.
The blackrobed one's *tsk*
as we refuse to enter his church, go our own way.
Bare feet circling stones,
polished by the rub of generations.

VIII.   PROPHET

Midlands made him. Miler.
Servant of God; father;
bishop. A man flourishing.
Until the storm.
To survive, twisting,
transfiguring in another form.
Straddling two traditions;
spies the promised land.

X.   EXODUS

Lord in his dun
surrounded by clan,
cattle and sheep grazing,
crops trembling in summer haze,
stone-thumps as women wash.

Rumble of hooves,
whoosh of flames,
swishes of unsheathing,
shudders of dying,
viscera stench,
smouldering ash.

XI.   PLANTATION

Moon guides flight –
aching soles, ankles twisting
on rabbit holes hidden by night.
Burrowing beneath whin
till day fades again.
Supping from streams;
scrabbling in furrows
for turnips, *prutas*.
Fleeing east from fire and steel.
Snared one morning –
encircled by curious faces,
points of graipes.
Gutteral Dalriadan grunts.
But kind natures
adopt the emaciated one.
One Scot's daughter,
set to nurse him,
nourish him, bonds.
Her kith accept him.
He stands with them in their kirk
to the sparse rituals.
Their Lord grants tenancy.

Who Am I

II

THE OTHER SIDE...

Olive McGrath (neé Tilson), with her brothers,
Fermanagh, c.1940.

XII   PLANTING THE SEED

They were always Northmen:
drifting to Normandy in longships,
settling Chester for the Bastard.
With the next invasion west
they brought the new faith
from Halifax to Christ Church and Elphin,
congregated in Cavan.

XIII.   HENRY

Just a journeyman chaplain:
after Oxford, I left Heptonshall behind,
found a living in Rochdale,
till attached to the Earl Strafford.

The extra income was welcome.
When he was appointed Lord Lieutenant
the catch – I'd to go to Ireland with him.
Fortune did not let me want:

I was appointed Dean of Christ Church, Dublin,
Vice-Chancellor of Trinity College,
had conferred on me the see of Elphin.
Till the Irish began one of their seasonal rampages:

I became a refugee in Dewsbury.
I was so reduced, I'd to consecrate
a parlour, preaching to keep thirteen of a family –
a prelate diminished to country curate.

Soon, they'd walk or jiggle in carts
for miles to hear me speak on a Sunday.
Like Lot cast down, then raised again,
I didn't waver along faith's way.

XIV.   GING

She'd teeter ladylike in crinkled nylons,
tweed skirt and jacket, hat tight on grey hair.
Beside us on the backseat, we'd pinch hand skin
wrinkles that would take ages to resettle.
The aunt who reared our mother would come with us
on outings to the seaside or for Sunday tea
at some nearby hotel restaurant
where she'd sip, with little finger raised, a sherry.

Perhaps because her own son fell in the street
with a brain haemorrhage aged 16, she'd indulge me,
offer a paper bag of chocolate sweets.
She began leaving cooker rings on,
gave sovereigns to grocers, went into a home,
would greet me, "Don't let the buggers get you down!"

XV.   OUR WILLIE

His earliest memory –
gunmen storming into
the unlocked kitchen,
thundering upstairs,
crouching in darkness,
barrels through windows
to ambush Black and Tans
as he cowered under a bed.
The old man was a B Special,
but that didn't stop him
from being held in a cell overnight
on the way home from calling
with a brother at the homeplace
in Leggykelly, Cavan - now
just across the new border.

Navvying in Blackpool
in the hard Thirties,
marginally easier than labouring
in rural Ulster.
Joining up for the War,
tending blistered feet in Italy,
where grenades made fish float
in quiet glades
after mad moments,
frenzied hand-to-hand
when triggers only click.
Coming through security
at Aldergrove as a pensioner,
quips to the bag-searcher,
'*It wasn't like this
arriving back from Dunkirk.*'

XVI.   FOSTERLING

Your mother told you it was safer there,
though Fermanagh's flying boats were out of range,
yet they'd fly so low over Antrim
heading for Langford Lodge or to Blitz Belfast
you'd see the Luftwaffe pilot's faces.
You were the third girl, she'd a younger son,
she gave you to a sister-in-law who'd only one.

The Norse wanderlust kicking in,
you trained at Middlesex,
witnessing the processions as they buried the old King
and crowned the young Queen,
before sailing for New Zealand and the Ozzie outback
on a £10 passage
to tend victims of snakebites and tropical diseases
and to nurse Ned Kelly's nephew.
During a sojourn home, a young farmer
was keen, still you headed to America.
Acting Matron at the top coronary unit
in the Big Apple, you worked with
Kantrowitz, who missed out to Barnard
on the first transplant by three days,
developed pacemakers and stints.
When your father got the Big C
you went home to help him,
later you'd nurse that keen farmer
you married for half a lifetime,
who'd keel over on the sofa
more than one morning, flatline awhile,
though it would take seven coronaries
to get the better of him.

XVII.   THE OTHER SIDE

A churchyard with scarcely any other name
on the headstones than theirs,
huddled within the wall, all neatly tended,
no weeds sullying this plot. They have become
almost native now – the big Viking frame
got beefy on plenty; blond hair fretted white.
Still martial, still stumbling each Twelfth
to the moan of their own drum,
swords blinding silver in summer light,
high-hedged country roads resonating
with the sound of their self-aggrandisement,
insects and vermin briefly scurrying aside
as they tramp, celebrating survival,
till nature prevails.

III

ANCESTOR WORSHIP...

Lizzie and John Kirk McGrath, c.1918
(see page 34).

XVIII.   FIRST AND SECOND SAMUEL

"For the Lord will not forsake His people…" (1 Samuel 12.22); *"…the Lord repented Him of the evil and said to the angel that destroyed the people, 'It is enough. Stay now thine hand.'* (2 Samuel 24.16)

In the long summer morning,
in the still summer morning,
as the light shines more brightly
and the world is cool and comfortable,
the rasp,
the rasp and swish of steel on stone
as the hook
is sharpened
at the cottage door.

The scrape,
the scrape of wood on stone
as he rises from the stool;
the slap,
the smack of palm on flank
as the cow is dismissed.

Our land is not our own
our faith is not our own
our children are not legitimate
we are constrained
yet we stretch
we strain
we kick.

The rasp,
the rasp of steel on wood.
It is his father,
honing a pole's tip,
who now reaches into the thatch
above the door,
withdraws the spike
hammered by the sweating smith
down in the glen
between horseshoes,
between visits of spying militiamen,
one of the pikeheads secreted,
passed under cover of straw and darkness,
point glistening
as head is bound to shaft
in the long summer morning,
in the still summer morning.

He reaches to take it
but his father holds back;
within, a baby cries,
a woken toddler moans at the door,
the young mother calls,

watching as the old man
shoulders pike and slashhook,
grim face mirroring grim face
watching as the aged peasant
stumbles along the path
towards the meeting place,
stumbles towards the town
in the long summer morning,
in the still summer morning.

XIX.   AGAINST THE TIDE

1840s
First chill of autumn on his breath,
he stoops to fork a top,
scatters loam, flinches
when the stench of rot assaults,
pus oozing from shells; gathers,
pockets the few miniscule tubers,
a youngster gurning at the halfdoor
as his father once did.

1890s
Still gaunt, this time age not hunger
has sapped bones, but he's strong enough
in summer warmth to strip to longjohns,
splits through the lint hole's
silver surface on his eightieth birthday
with a breaststroke and a shriek!

XX.   ANCESTOR WORSHIP

A candle flickers on the deep window sill
in the drystone byre as his hands
draw warm strones from the udder, cow shifting
from hoof to hoof in her new home.
Thus, first nights can be like any other.

Except for the clatter of hooves outside
and thud of stick on the top-half of the door.
Raised voices.
Lizzie panicking, nyerking child swinging,
to her apron clinging.

The lord's agent's demanding a month's rent
in advance, wants it in the morning.
He barks at her to go back into the house,
not upraise the beast, he's had to rise
from the stool with the pail to avoid her dancing rump.
Thumping her to milk again face clenched
against her flank, inspiration strikes.

He treads all night over the hills
to McFadden's, arrives with the frost, boots torn,
is called in by the gentleman to breakfast,
to explain *whatever's wrong?* is given
the money he needs to avoid eviction –
repay when you can –
spare boots, the loan of a horse home –
reciprocation for some past good turn.

In his sixties, drying grain, turning a shovel shaft
on his knee, which will graze and bleed,
the onset of diabetes brings gangrene.
The doctor's fee's a golden guinea –
he protests too long, *it's nothing*.
Lizzie ends her ninetynine years
under a duncher in the chimney corner,
clay pipe between her lips, eyes bright
as a cat's in the shade of a hedge
when one of her eleven offspring stops by.

XXI.   WILLIE JOHN

The master delivered him home
from school in a cart,
flummoxed he couldn't get the boy
to read or write.
Eight years old, Willie John enjoyed
work on the farm.

Evenings, his grandfather would claim
he couldn't see
newsprint by candlelight,
coaxed the child to read to him.
Land League stories
burned bright.

He'd cycle one Sunday with his son
fifteen miles to march
the black heathered hill;
from a callbox, did the deal,
borrowing the cash
the next morning at nine.

XXII.   COVENANT

Picture Carson in Edwardian frock coat
stooped at the table signing,
a quarter of a million men joining
him. And a quarter of a million
women had their own Declaration,
some using their blood as ink on the Covenant.

In the Public Records collection
I locate my grandmother's signature
and, beside it, her mother's.
It must've been a special day in Stranocum,
banners fluttering against azure
sky, a time of celebration.

Cassie was a stripling, of course,
knew nothing of what lay ahead:
how she'd be in O'Connell Street,
one of the bemused as Pearse
unscrolled *his* declaration, read
and the world shuddered on its pivot.

How, at a dance, she'd meet
a freethinking lad, vow
to be his wife; learn
other shades of green;
and that pledges made in the heat
of the moment don't always ring true.

XXIII.   CASSIE

A coffin-maker's daughter – that dimly-lit
workshop behind the terraced-house in Stranocum,
sawdust curls on the concrete, shelves of made-to-fit
boxes around the walls – I was struck dumb
by your fervid kiss as the strains of fiddle and accordion
thumped from the parlour; relatives and neighbours chattering;
floorboards reverberating beneath everyone's
partying; the lightness of your eyelashes fluttering
against my cheek. Home from Dublin, where you kept
court at a counter in Clery's; only departing
when Easter's street mayhem erupts.
Yet all the local women come cycling:
farmers' wives, engaged girls, magnetised
by the same, as you'd say, *joie de vivre*, that captivated me.
The series of maids you hired – my mother never needed
such extravagance – times you exasperated me.

I see you struggling across the yard, shoulders
hunched beneath the weight of metal buckets -
slopping against your apron as if our demanding childer -
like that other Catherine, burdened by the wheel of a cart.
I still never caught on, caught myself on,
when you had the miscarriage, it might've been something
to do with two-handled pots on the range, steel brutes
boiling veg, braising meat, long hours spud-dropping
and turnip-thinning in damp fields that got
to you. And when the youngsters fell to fever
sleepless nights by their beds nursing had its effect.
I thought I'd have you forever,
never imagined you'd be the one to succumb to the scarlet...
Friends walk with me through November chill,
sing solemnly - not merrily, like you at our wedding supper -
wreaths stretch to the crest of the hill.
When I lift your coffin it's light as a feather.

XXIV.   BELONGING

Not the wicked stepmother Dad recalls
who terrified his brother, warped grey cells:
she was disappointed by some young man,
she took him to court, but he denied the wean –
some mates cutely claimed she was a whore
who'd slept with them. In service, scrubbing floors
in some Big House – her baby adopted –
her sister died – Ruby surrogated:
housekeeper-wife, she went on honeymoon
with her niece, now new daughter, Marion.
Willie John stayed home, pared ploughhorses' hooves,
hammered zinc sheets on byre and stable roofs.
On Christmas Day, while Dad and his siblings
were at the church service, she'd take their things –
she'd leave only an orange in each sock,
the rest, rewrapped for her child to unpack.
By Mummy's time they had tablets for it:
Ruby had to thole hot flushes, night sweats;
wandering country roads babbling, mood swings,
snapping, lashing out at the kids, scowling.
Once, when depression struck, she just didn't return;
she found a house near her own, settled down.

XXV.   THE DARKEST HOUR

Snow was general all over Ireland.
In the black north, above the black city,
the Black Mountain was transformed white.
but the blackface sheep lay
under the weight of death,
lips black, eyes black, noses cold, limbs stiff.

John had just come of age.
As they dug a handful of survivors from gullies
to shiver in a trailer as winter wind
sliced round hillsides like a *skean dhu*,
he noticed for the first time
how his Da's back had become age-bent.
Slumping into the cab, wiping his brow,
John's pectoral muscle spasmed as
he voiced his loss – hundreds
beneath deep drifts.
The quaver of his words reminding him
of the time the old man knelt
in muck in the byre to plead
with, for the only time in his life,
tears in his eyes, for him not to
go off to the war but stay and help him.
And now, with the light of dark clouds
reflecting off frozen hills,
his Da muttered, "I started with nothing
afore. This time, I've got you to help me."
With a key turn, the lorry's ignition
spluttered, the engine roared.

XXVI.   ALAN

They'd just got back from a week at the Port,
lads in Fifties suits.
Alan had done the chores for his brother –
as well as feeding sows
he'd sat on a stool, head against the cow's
flank. She was cantankerous,
sent milk spilling with a kick.
The cleft hoof caught his groin.
He'd stumbled into the house,
hands clasped before bloody trousers.
The doctor clean him up, stitched the scrotum.
Later, he'd claim it wasn't the cause
of Alan's hallucinations – tossing an iron
through a window pane at some girl's
feuding brothers, chasing sister Betty
down the back loanen to the rill
with a graipe, slashing his brother's ear
with a billhook, because *they* were threatening…
Perhaps an explanation lay years back
in his stepmother's menstrual frenzies
or within the brain's unfathomable creases.
The field would nearly be baled
before he'd rise from the dyke, stook
like a madman, to catch up with the tractor,
chainsmoking till lungs turned
as black as his stare.

XXVII.   VISION

Strains of *Be Thou My Vision* commence
as your coffin is wheeled into the hall
of the funeral parlour.
A few days hence, I wheeled your latest grandson,
a few days old, into the sitting room
and you slipped a score in the sleeping child's pram.
As we bow our heads to pray
you'd have a wry smile
at the spider scurrying on the wall
and skirting board like a louse on someone's hat.
The spider's so busy she's a blur –
like your father in that photo they called him
from ploughing to take, because sisters
were visiting from the States.
You would approve of this insect's disregard
for social niceties, her preference
for getting things done -
none of this fruitless speculation,
interminably seeking the kernel,
as we follow you on your final journey -
floating to the centre on a flimsy thread.

IV

WHO DO YOU THINK YOU ARE…?

Cassie's children: Betty, Marion, John and Alan, 1930s

XXVIII.   AN ULSTER NATIVITY

"It is a wind which carries the seeds of life and the dust of extinction… It is a winnowing wind. It is a bitter wind."
(Campbell McGrath, *"Langdon, North Dakota"*)

I

March wind shivering in his heart,
with flickering evenings of stars
and clouds of breath blowing against his shirt,
alone in the yard, squinting to bounce over bars
of a gate, as he hoists liths of straw
from mouths, moaning calves bucking
against him, hooves pressing on boots like claws,
always one with lips keenly finger-sucking.

II

Now, it's all only a December ache, flooding
on the breeze of nostalgia as he sniffs manure:
how he knelt before the hearth, parcels thudding
promisingly of Lego or some remote-controlled car
which never came. That one light on the plastic tree
winking: a dead brother's whispered glee.

XXIX.   GROUNDKEEPERS
(*"Eliminate groundkeepers, as they harbour disease",
Dept of Agriculture advice brochure*)

Thon wee ones, Da called them; referring
to family lore, those who survived the famine
by secreting these tiny *prutas* in pockets.
Ammunition. Seed that would see them through the worst.
My patch of potatoes cannot match their struggle.
And when I turn up tuber specks but
don't salvage, chuck them with the waste, in my stomach
there stalks an ancient hunger.

XXX.   NAME CALLING
        "Sticks and stones may break my bones…"

It was a teacher in England
who kept badgering me,
"So that's a *Catholic* name?"

It was an Ulster novelist
who pointed out over a pint there'd been
a trend among upwardly mobile Prods
in the era of his prime, the Sixties,
to give their offspring Irish names.

There was the policeman
Dad would have a whiskey with,
who did point duty at Carlisle Circus,
who gave his son the same name;

and the archbishop's doctor son
I saw interviewed on TV once.

The time I was helping a neighbour shift cattle
on conacre land in North Down,
a well-to-do farmer helping us there,
on hearing my name, commented,
"like Niall of the Nine Hostages."
When I acknowledged the legend
he demanded,
"How do *you* know about *him*?"
I was unable to articulate then
my history-buff father's
enthusiasm after a trip to Tara.

I'd learn how MacNeice considered himself
'A Protestant with a Fenian name'.
Perhaps not quite the same for him in peacetime
or at boarding school across the water
as for me growing up during the Troubles,
one side suspicious because of the name,
the other at first open, then clamming up
on discovering you weren't 'one of them'.

But my sister-in-law, reared within the Pale,
beats Banaher: preparing for her Baptism,
the priest refused to refer to her by
the first name her mother chose,
called her, in his Jansenistic wisdom,
by her saintly middle name, 'Anne',
rather than use the pagan 'Deirdre'.

XXXI.   CLAY

Spading over the vegetable patch
this year instead of my father watching
the toddlers are with me, play like Krishna
and Balaram: one sprays soil with a toy shovel,
the other is perched on his tricycle.
One gurns as if I were mother Yasoda:
the wee one is eating earth.
I wipe his face clean with a hankie,
see the gleam in his eye,
an entire universe in his mouth.

XXXII.   WHERE BONES COME FROM

More awesome even than the birds and the bees,
I walk hand-in-hand down the field with my son
who, in his four year old-wisdom shrills,
"So that's where bones come from!" as I explain

how a fox has killed the lamb; how the body
decays, matter and soul recycle.
He wants to know where Grandad lives now:
"In the heavenly plane..." I theorise about the spiritual.

But he interrupts, babbles about loving birds,
what a marvellous home a nest is!
how he recalls flitting from branch to branch;
leaves me lost for words,
bowing to give whitethorn a kiss,
giggles at a primrose, clutching his paunch.

*'Tha boyz' with their Grannie McGrath, c.2008 – see
'Clay', 'Fosterling' and 'Where Bones Come From'*

'Cassie': Catherine McGrath, c.1918

NOTES ON *WHO I AM*

Introduction

This sequence is an attempt to present significant moments in my family history. Originally, the concept centred around the idea of 'Ancestor Worship', but as others (most notably Michael S Begnal) have used that title, I searched for another. Thus, the currently popular television series about tracing ancestral roots, *Who Do You Think You Are?*, has inspired the more definite title of this sequence, *Who I Am*. The suggestion is, of course, that the experiences of forebears shape the individual as well as our own experiences.

Structure

The sequence begins with a series of poems on prehistory – basically from the creation. It mirrors Biblical legends initially, such as the flood. The first section covers the period until the Plantation of Ulster, when my modern family history, in my mind, begins. By this, I mean my 'clan', that is, the paternal or McGrath side. Family lore has it that the 'Ur' McGrath fled their Pettigo kingdom (Castle McGrath still stands there, albeit in ruins, in South Donegal) east, settling with Scottish Presbyterian planters in the Braid Valley, County Antrim. The tenancy at Cloneytrace was passed down from eldest son to eldest son, until my great-grandfather (John Kirk McGrath) took advantage of the coming Land Acts (late 1800s) to take a tenancy of his own near Antrim. My grandfather and father also moved to new farms in the area. All were eldest sons, as I am, so the legend is that we are eldest sons all the way back to the early 1600s. This is, of course, oral tradition - there are no written records as evidence. Ironically, as a student some years ago I worked one summer as a postman in the Broughshane area and delivered the mail to the 'ancestral' house my great-great-grandfather had lived in, where my great-grandfather was born and reared.

The second section focuses on my mother's side of my background, the Tilsons, from County Fermanagh, who came to Ulster as planters, and traces them to the present day. Unfortunately, I know less about this side of the family.

The third section picks up the story at the time of the 1798 rebellion, which my Presbyterian forefathers (McGraths) were involved in. This section recounts significant moments in the lives of my nearest ancestors, as we reach 'living memory'. These stories were, of course, related to me by my late father and other relatives.

I include a final section focussing on the future as much as myself, in that I include my sons in the sequence. My wife's family, from County Kildare, feature to a small extent in one piece, given that this aspect of the history is part of my sons' background.

'Our Willie' Tison, 1993, Australia
(see page 26).

The poems

    i. Genesis – This piece mirrors the Biblical story of creation, starting with the end of the last ice age, when Northern Europe emerged from beneath glaciers and could be said to have been a cultural and spiritual 'blank canvas'. *'Beyond the memory of man'* – i.e. 'prehistory' – the phrase is from Chaucer. This piece therefore traces human origins 70,000 years ago in Africa to their spread across the globe, to Ireland. The island's uninhabited status gives way to settlement by Neolithic adventures.

    ii. Expulsion – The Eden of the Bible was a river valley plain, with Neolithic people settling and becoming farmers for the first time, and that 'industry' and production of surpluses created the first 'civilisation', but also the first experiences of greed and jealousy. The Hebrew word for the 'tree of the knowledge of good and evil' also means 'vine', hence references in this piece to drink (which can cause break-ups of families/relationships).

Cain was an arable farmer and so 'good' (as meat production is seen in this context as unholy), but poor; Abel farmed sheep and 'supplies' the lust for wealth (presumably through wool production – ancient Judaic texts suggest there was no 'industrial' production of meat until after the Flood) - which here is seen as spiritually 'bad'. Abel's being blessed with material riches creates jealousy in Cain, who kills Abel and so is banished from the spiritual Eden or paradise. Cain's parents (Adam and Eve - an idealised couple) are also later expelled, for craving material things and succumbing to carnal desires (vanity, as well as sexual indulgence). The phrase *'Like Dolmens round my childhood the old people'* is from John Montague's poem of that title.

    iii. Deluge – i.e. the Biblical (and post-ice age) flood. Symbolises the flood and also the 'new covenant' of blood, as the waterlogged land forces the 'good people' to abandon vegetarianism and resort to meat-eating to survive and, now they have the taste of blood, they continue to do so until the present day. Thus, the material plane of existence gains a foothold over the more spiritual.

iv. Of King and Country - Kennedy was the father of Brian Boru. One of Brian's brother's was Echtigern, the Horse Lord. His grandson was the first 'MagCraith' or 'McGrath' from which my family stems. When Vikings raided the clan settlement, only the eldest son of Kennedy, Mahon, and the youngest, Brian, survived.

v. After the Horse Lord – this poem is about Irish and Scottish families/clans and places named after Echtigern and his offspring.

vi. Holy Land – this piece is a musing on the female godhead of Irish lore – Epona, also known as Macha, the horse goddess. She symbolises also the fertility of the land. Hopefully, this comes across as a lyrical piece describing the society of the day. 'Sixmilebridge to Sixmilewater' suggests the spread of the McGrath clan / family name from the south to the north.

vii. Diaspora - this poem is about the pre-plantation spread of 'clans' McGrath.

viii. Keepers of the Lough – Pre-plantation, the McGrath clan, kings of South Donegal based at McGrath Castle at Pettigo, were guardians for the Church of Lough Derg, Co Donegal. The form of this poem is a reversed or inverted sonnet, which is aimed at mirroring the form of part 'X' in "Station Island" by Heaney. Other poetic devices used in this piece are: intertextual references include, in stanza 3, the word "cornflower" which is originally used by Heaney; in line 12, an extra stress is added; in lines 13 & 14 the stresses are reversed (4/3 – 3/4) to suggest change but continuity. The stones are originally pagan and so older than the church (especially, the Jansenistic phase of Irish Catholicism which recently has controlled the Lough). Derg was written about by Kavanagh and others as well as Heaney. This piece considers my own visit to Derg, when I did not accept the priest's offer to attend a service.

ix. Prophet – this piece is about Bishop Miler McGrath (c.1523-1623?). He was both a Roman Catholic and Church of Ireland bishop at the same time, as well as being a family man. His life is indicative of a time when many had to make compromises and move with the flow of events and history in order to survive and prosper.

x. Exodus – this poem is about the violence of the Plantation of Ulster, which swept away the old Celtic feudal system.

xi. Plantation – The 'Ur' McGrath of our family moves from Donegal to Antrim, fleeing after dispossession during the plantation. This poem shows how he came to settle with the Scottish planters in Co. Antrim.

xii. Planting the Seed – this first piece of the second section is about my mother's family (Tilsons), moving from Scandinavia via Normandy to England and Ireland. The term 'Northmen' was used by the Anglo-Saxons in 1066 to describe the Normans. Ironically, this family have moved from Northern Europe (Scandinavia), to Northern France (Normandy), to the North of England and thence to the North of Ireland.

xiii. Henry – this piece is about a famous son of the family – Bishop Henry Tilson (1600s). Initially, he profited from the Plantation, but soon fell foul of the powers that be and ended his days relatively destitute, back in the North of England.

xiv. Ging – the title of this poem was a pet name my sister and I had when we were small for the aunt who brought up my mother, in Antrim (see Fosterling below).

xv. Our Willie – about my mother's eldest brother, who fought in the Second World War – at Dunkirk, Italy etc., and later settled in Australia.

xvi. Fosterling – this poem is about my mother.

xvii. The Other Side – this last piece of the second section is a general piece about my mother's family in rural Fermanagh, where the Protestant population has dwindled.

xviii. 1st & 2nd Samuel – this piece is about the Insurrection of 1798. It is about two Samuel McGraths, father and son, from that time. Family lore is that the younger Samuel was to go with the Presbyterian (and Roman Catholic) rebels to fight in the Battle of Antrim, but on the morning his father reasoned with him that he should go, as he was older and so it did not matter so much if he were killed, whereas the younger Samuel had a young family to support.

xix. Against the Tide – the later poem called Groundkeepers is about same subject as this one – the Potato Famine of the 1840s. The shriek at the end of this piece is one of exhilaration and joy, not only of the immediate achievement - of William John's swimming the cold lint hole (where flax would be steeped) on his eightieth birthday - but also at their having come through, survived hard times.

xx. Ancestor Worship – this poem is about the generation born approx. 1858/9 – chiefly John Kirk (my great-grandfather) and his wife, Lizzie White. He died in the early 1920s, she in the late 1950s. When the Land League agitation led to tenants being allowed to buy the land from the Lords, my great-grandfather moved to a new farm (from the 'ancestral' one) in order that he would have a farm of his own, as well as (presumably, his father and a brother or sister) retaining the original tenancy place in the family. This piece recounts how, on the first night in the new farm, eviction threatened. John Kirk was lent the initial rent money by someone he knew, which meant that he and his young family avoided eviction. John Kirk's son (Willie John) and grandson, my father, John, managed to go on to succeed at farming, none of which would have been possible had it not been for that act of kindness.

xxi. Willie John – this poem is about my paternal grandfather and how he prospered as a farmer, despite leaving school aged eight.

xxii. Covenant – this piece is about my paternal grandmother, her mother and family, from Stranocum, in County Antrim. It is about the Loyalist Covenant that women signed in 1912.

xxiii. Cassie – this poem is about my paternal grandmother. It is told from the point of view of my grandfather (Willie John, her husband), as she died in 1929 when my father was small and so he never really knew her. Some years ago I was teaching poetry workshops in schools as part of an Arts Council of Northern Ireland scheme. While at St Catherine's Primary School, Falls Road, Belfast, I suggested the pupils could write about someone they know, such as their grandmothers, or someone famous, such as the St Catherine the school was named after. Having set this onerous task, I realised I should set an example and write one myself – so (while staying in the Citywest Hotel, County Dublin) I wrote this poem about my grandmother, Catherine.

xxiv. Belonging – this self-explanatory poem is about the troubled life of my father's stepmother, Ruby (also his aunt, and Cassie's sister).

xxv. The Darkest Hour – this poem is about the deep snow of the winter of 1947. My father and grandfather had sheep grazing on Belfast's Black Mountain and virtually lost the lot under the snow. That is, the family faced destitution again, after the hungry years of the 20s/30s that Willie John had to lead his family through. Willie John's stoicism helped my father cope.

xxvi. Alan – this poem is about my schizophrenic uncle (John's brother).

xxvii. Vision – this piece is about my father's funeral and the birth of my second son which ocurred withn a week. Also, it is about my father's legacy – his 'vision' – and his work ethic.

xxviii. The final section - Who do you think you are? - focusses on my own life – and "the future" i.e. my children. I wanted this sequence to be mainly about the 'ancestors', but felt a nod to the present and future was necessary. An Ulster Nativity – this first piece is a meditation upon my own childhood growing up on the family farm and the brother who died as a baby and so only saw one Christmas with us.

xxix. Groundkeepers – see the piece 'Against the Tide' above – this poem is a meditation on my own gardening – growing potatoes - in relation to the poverty experienced by ancestors, especially during the potato famine.

xxx. Name Calling – this piece is about some of my experiences of the Troubles and sectarianism. Also, it aims to embrace my own family, that is, my children's 'other side', my in-laws from Kildare. The sequence is completed as being inclusive in that is moves from the Irish Catholic origins, through the adoption of Presbyterianism, the planter aspect, through to my wife and I being of 'mixed' backgrounds – Northern Protestant and Southern Catholic – while having separately adopted and sharing a Vaisnavist perspective.

xxxi. Clay – this poem is similar to 'Groundkeepers', as it is about digging in the garden (the plot where, in the past, I would have grown potatoes and vegetables with my father).

xxxii. Where Bones Come From – the "bones" suggest 'ancestor worship', and the fact that we all end up in the earth/clay as bones. This piece is a meditation on the eternally difficult question of life and death and how to answer these fundamental questions (what does it all mean? is this all there is?) for ourselves, as well as when posed by a child. It considers reincarnation (through the adult's theorising and the child's tale of having been a bird – real or imagined?). The child's reaction, to become a 'laughing buddha', shows how the child can be father of the man, and how we can cope with the often terrifying prospects of death and uncertainty.

Niall McGrath
County Antrim
November 2009

Niall McGrath

Krishna - Protector of Cows

Niall McGrath

Who Am I